Stephanie Kwolek
and Bulletproof Material

By Ellen Labrecque

21st Century
Junior Library

Published in the United States of America by
Cherry Lake Publishing
Ann Arbor, Michigan
www.cherrylakepublishing.com

Content Adviser: Amelia Wenk Gotwals, Ph.D., Associate Professor of Science Education, Michigan State University
Reading Adviser: Marla Conn MS, Ed., Literacy specialist, Read-Ability, Inc.

Photo Credits: © FeyginFoto/Shutterstock Images, cover; © 1000 Words/Shutterstock Images, 4; © Chemical Heritage
Foundaction, Harry Kalish/Wikimedia (Mary Mark Ockerbloom), 6; © Everett Historical/Shutterstock Images, 8; © AngelPet/
Shutterstock Images, 10; © DuPont, 12; © TLaoPhotography/Shutterstock Images, 14; © NA image/Shutterstock Images, 16; ©
JTKPHOTO/Shutterstock Images, 18; © DuPont, 20

Library of Congress Cataloging-in-Publication data on file.

Cherry Lake Publishing would like to acknowledge the work of The Partnership for 21st Century Skills.
Please visit *www.p21.org* for more information.

Printed in the United States of America
Corporate Graphics

CONTENTS

Police officers protect the public.

A Woman

Police officers have an important job. They help people in emergencies. Their work can be dangerous. Sometimes people shoot at them. Thankfully, they can be protected by special clothing.

Stephanie Kwolek is the scientist who **invented Kevlar**. Kevlar is a bulletproof material. It has the power to stop speeding bullets! It is used to make helmets and vests.

Stephanie became interested in science because
she loved nature.

Stephanie Kwolek was born on July 31, 1923, in New Kensington, Pennsylvania. Her dad, John, and mom, Nellie, were **immigrants** from Poland. Stephanie's mom taught her to sew.

Stephanie's dad worked in a factory. But he loved the outdoors. He took his daughter on many trips to explore the woods and fields.

Think!

Kwolek said her trips into the woods made her curious! Why do you think this is the case? Have you learned things from being in the woods? Or from just exploring outside?

During World War II, DuPont made lifesaving
parachutes for American pilots.

Stephanie went to Carnegie Mellon University in Pittsburgh, Pennsylvania. She studied **chemistry**. She graduated in 1946. After college, she worked as a research scientist in a **laboratory**. She worked for DuPont. DuPont is a company that invents materials for things such as tires and **parachutes**.

Tires wear out. When they are no longer safe, they must be replaced.

In 1965, when Kwolek was 42, she began working on a new material. She wanted to invent a tough material that would help tires last for years. Instead, she invented a material that was even tougher and lighter than anybody thought possible!

Create!

Pretend you could invent a new material. What would it be? For example, would it be a special kind of blanket that never got wet?

Kevlar can be spun into fibers like these.

An Idea

Stephanie Kwolek had invented a liquid. She put the liquid into a machine. She spun it into a superstrong material. Kwolek discovered that this material was five times stronger than steel! Steel is one of the strongest metals there is. DuPont named it Kevlar.

Kevlar fibers can be woven into fabric.

Kwolek and a team of scientists did many tests on Kevlar. They discovered that Kevlar is flexible but strong. It is not easily broken. It does not melt under hot or cold conditions. It is also very light.

Ask Questions!

Ask your teacher or librarian about uses of Kevlar. Can they tell you more about it? Do some research about Kevlar on the Internet.

Many layers of Kevlar are woven and sealed together
to make a bulletproof vest.

A Legacy

Other scientists tested Kevlar. They quickly discovered that Kwolek's invention could be used to make bulletproof vests. Police officers wear these vests all over the world. To honor the lives saved by Kwolek's invention, DuPont created a survivor's club. The club is for police officers whose lives were saved by Kevlar. Saving their lives is Stephanie Kwolek's **legacy**.

Some tennis rackets are strung with Kevlar for extra strength.

Today, Kevlar is also used to make fun things like baseball bats and tennis rackets. Sometimes it is even used to make athletic shoes. Kevlar makes this equipment lighter and safer.

Kwolek used chemistry to save thousands of lives.

Kwolek was inducted into the National Inventors Hall of Fame in 1994. She died on June 18, 2014, at age 90. She spent her career working for DuPont. "There are thousands of people alive because of her," a police chief said about Kwolek. Her discovery continues to help people every day!

GLOSSARY

chemistry (KEM-uh-stree) the scientific study of substances, what they are composed of, and how they react with each other

immigrants (IM-ih-gruhnts) people who move from one country to another and settle there

invented (in-VENT-id) created something new from imagination

Kevlar (KEV-lahr) a plastic strong enough to stop bullets and knives from getting through it

laboratory (LAB-ruh-tor-ee) a room or building that has special equipment for people to use to do scientific experiments

legacy (LEG-uh-see) something handed down from one generation to another

parachutes (PA-ruh-shoots) large pieces of strong but lightweight fabric attached to thin ropes that spread out in the air to slow the descent of whatever is attached to them

FIND OUT MORE

BOOKS

Stewart, Gail. *Stephanie Kwolek: Creator of Kevlar*. Detroit: KidHaven Press, 2009.

Waisman, Charlotte. *Her Story: A Timeline of the Women Who Changed America*. New York: HarperCollins, 2008.

Wyckoff, Edwin Brit. *The Woman Who Invented the Thread That Stops Bullets: The Genius of Stephanie Kwolek*. Berkeley Heights, NJ: Enslow Publishing, 2014.

WEB SITES

Explain That Stuff!—Kevlar
www.explainthatstuff.com/kevlar.html
Learn more about how Kevlar works.

National Inventors Hall of Fame
http://invent.org
Find out more about Stephanie Kwolek and other famous inventors.

INDEX

ABOUT THE AUTHOR

Ellen Labrecque is a freelance writer living in Yardley, Pennsylvania. Previously, she was a senior editor at Sports Illustrated Kids. Ellen loves to travel and then learn about new places and people that she can write about in her books.